LEADERS LEADING THE WAY

ISBN 9781521025055

INTRODUCTION

As you start reading you will discover things that Ricky and I have experience during the course of our journey together being processed and developed as a leader. We have encountered many seasons of training, building, equipping, developing, leading, mentoring, being mentored, struggles, victories, what to do and what not to do, but really learning some importance of leadership, self- development and knowing what to do with what you have.

As you remember in your history classes or learning moments at home, leaders where discussed, examined, tried, tested, honored, and even appreciated. Leaders of many cultures teaching different ways and leaders of many spiritual beliefs empowering different moves! One thing for sure God has created us all and placed greatness in us all to share with the world. Now how and what we do with it is up to the person involved.

Our desire is that you will come to the place of operating as a leader doing things the way the Lord has created us to be known as, CREATION OF HIS IMAGE AND LIKENESS!

Our hope is that this book excites you, active your gifts, bring awareness to you, encourage you, empower you, build you, and catapult you to a position of leading. For the spirit of the Lord is restoring, bringing forth, rising up, and transitioning leaders all over the world! So there is room for you to expand more, lead more, save more, heal more, develop more, launch more, and release more people into their places here in the earth!

You are needed and your voice and experiences with the Lord does matter.

Table of Contents

LEADING WITH YOUR STRENGTHS

One job of every person is to be yourself be all that you can be. You have strengths that relate to your character and personality. Strengths of your life will create goals, visions, dreams, innovations, strategies, and encouragement to yourself and others. There are things and ideas that you do that others will not ever do like you. Your strengths you have will allow you to build people and encourage them. By releasing ideas to people for accomplishments, help you to relate to other people in every element in life, and your strengths also bring you around people that are helpful to you as well. When you realize what your strengths are you will be amazed at what you can do for others as in strengthening and helping them accomplish goals. You can look at strengths like this, "you being capable of knowing what you can do"; in life for yourself and for others it will just leap out of you! Now please know this, you having strengths does not mean no one else in life or no one else around you has strengths to offer. Having a desire to help others find their strengths and affirm them in their abilities to function in them is a real leader with great character for leading people. This is awesome to use as what you bring to the team or bring to people as a "gift", and not ever having a need to be selfish with what you offer others. I know, right? Can you just imagine for a moment, the people you are leading, or the people that are on the team you are on, or you and your family look at how powerful and unstoppable you are using your strengths together to get the job done or to complete a task that is at hand or even to achieve any goals that have been set! This is a sure way of finishing strong! This is also a great way to know who you work and labor with to develop things, build businesses, and have an incredible plan for others to follow. Amazing right? Exactly the point I'm making today. I want you to know it is okay that you were not shown your strengths. You were probably like me just told what to do all the time and that was the best way to do it period! Well that works only for so long. The input of others and using listening skills to hear what people are really saying as well as listening with discernment in place to know what people are saying when they really are not talking about it! For example, when I would teach a song to the choir and some of the people would sing whatever they wanted to instead of the part I would give them to sing. I would get upset and be disappointed and I would just let them just sing it however you want right now. But I really know you can do better than what you are giving me so I'm tired of trying to get you to understand your talent is bigger than what you are singing like. So I just settled with what they gave. Until one day I needed to be honest but only to the point of expressing my concerns of their singing with the idea of doing better looks like this, "sounding better will produce a quality of this kind of effect." When I decided to change my behavior to improve the choir's outcome of greatness I needed to show them that I cared with a different sound in my speech. It is the same when you lead people you must know the people and know how to connect with the people and show them how you care with sounding like you do care! You will be able to read more about connecting with people you lead and love later on in the book. I have great information and experiences in this book I believe will empower, equip, develop, ignite, activate, challenge your mind to change, and encourage you to be all that you desire! Hope you are hungry for more, please let's go on!

Being a leader is not just positional it is about being functional. Leadership is work! You can lead all by yourself, but how effective will that be? Leading people, a company, a vision, a project, or a promise takes consistency to apply oneself to the job and to engage with the people that are involved with making things happen! Holding the positon of "leader" is not about telling people what to do. It is showing people how to do it. Modeling what you are, "a leader leading the way"! Good moral character, relational, personality, healthy attitude, sensitive and flexible to the Lord, and good communication skills. The leader is a person who chooses to make healthy decisions for the whole group as well as listen to the group. I remember a story about this pastor who could preach you up out of your seats! He could sing the right songs at the right time to encourage people to join. It was so exciting to see him in action! However when it came to showing the people how to live what they heard him preach Sunday after Sunday wasn't going well for him because he really did not know how to give the congregants a true example outside of the church himself. His understanding of pastoring the people was preaching the gospel well and that was all it took. But as he began to see the image he created was not effective to a changed life in Christ! The pastor only preached the gospel to show a position of leading. The pastor never lived the gospel which could have given him a functional role as a leader. It's easy to talk about what you should do or tell people this is the way to live and yet you have not tried the formula of life for your own self. "When your destiny in God is bigger than your desire how you think about your life. It will come to a point in your life where you will need to crossover to another side in your life to produce the next phase of your life! "From probability to possibility"! Knowing your desire to be and to do will help create a hunger to produce what you are becoming! I like this saying, "feed what you believe"! When you eat from true resources then you will flourish in the things you are really hungry for. If you believe that you are a leader, you will find ways to help yourself improve so you can improve others to do great. In the book of Daniel, he talks about the people that know their God shall do great exploits! Sometimes you must build yourself strong and encourage yourself to do great things because greatness is in you.

The word encouragement says something that makes someone more determined, hopeful, or confident. When a leader boost the team to achieve their goals and give incentives to complete their task, or even speak well of their outcome of communicating with the people and with the team shows you notice the good work and ideas they do and bring to the team. Expressing how you appreciate their ideas and work helps your congregation, team, leadership, and family with positive words spoken rather than harsh words allows a healthy relationship grow and flourish. Giving affirmations to people you believe in, people you are in relationship with, people that are a part of your team, and even people you display your leadership skills to. I remember my girls in elementary school. Their school had just got a report about the children's test scores were too low, and the problem must be fixed or the school would be in a position of closing. So I went to the principal and ask how can I pray for the leadership? What was her plan to change things at the school? When she gave me the information I immediately created a strategy with a plan to follow. I went to the ministers of the church that Ricky and I pastored, and showed them the strategy and asked who could help and where they could apply themselves to the plan. Afterwards I went to the school and put the plan to work, now it took work and people being involved but I was determined that success would come from it for the sake of our children and their education. Once everyone at the school was on board we placed a minister with every teacher to aid and assist them. Next we helped in the office with any and all things to show them we appreciated them. Another session we were allowed to facilitate their team meeting. I was so excited to have a great meeting so I had two other ministers go with me to help me help them. We had refreshments for them. We knew they would be tired from a long day with the children and the pressure they were feeling getting the scores improved with the children. So along with refreshments we gave free massages to the teachers, office workers, and principals anyone that was willingly. We created an atmosphere of encouragement to each other. We give appreciation for their hard work. We used group activities of learning from each other to aid in team work for effectiveness. All of these things to relax them and give them momentum to continue the great work! As well as that went following after the event they all starting talking to each other differently and realized they were all in this challenge together and it would take them working together and working with us helping them reach their goals would produce the greater effect. Just to show you how this behavior became contagious. One of the ministers at the church which was in a leading role, she finds information for each person that was helping with our tutoring project. She got paperwork through an organization for each tutor to sign in with how many hours they tutored in the week. With that said, they tutored children from the school and other schools and their hours were used as payment to their existing and past student loans. So I used strengths I had but didn't know they were my strengths and the other ministers used theirs as well. It was just a hunger to create a plan to solve a problem! With an ability to create, I guess I needed to do it and they needed something done! But the most beautiful impressive point was this, it ignited everyone that was working together and as they shared the news with other people those people were ignited with excitement, hope, desires awaken, encouragement to their situations, and just about anything that could happen was happening for the good! And the end of that story goes like this. The test scores at the school improved and the school did not close. The principle's goal was completed and everyone even the children was a success! Stop focusing on what you or the people can't do. Start looking at how you can plan something good and different. How you can build the excitement back into your team. How you can be a part of your team. How you will empower people, ignite people, active people, impart into people. What will it look like? How will you sound to them? What will you use different to connect with them? When you finish teaching, training, preaching, will they leave your presence having a new personal experience?

Christ looked at our strengths when He chose us! Building people on their strengths is creative ability of Christ. Now that's a model to look at for leadership. He speaks to us from His heart to our capabilities without doubting if we can do it! Let's look at how Christ functioned as a leader. He used the servant concept. He didn't think of himself greater or higher up than anyone He ministered to. He had a heart for people. He modeled relationship continually. He showed them how to be leaders among the people. He fellowshipped, ate and fed the people. He came to us to serve not be served. He lived in respect of people and in willingness to forgive and love. Christ does not focus only on our sin, short comings, and negativity. He focuses on achieving the goal He was given by fulfilling His destiny with blessing the people and meeting their unmet needs. He lived out what He was called to do, "lead the way"! He knew He had to train leaders to take on His behavior and the leaders had to learn that what they saw Christ do is what they must endure to do.

Give the best you have don't quit or give up! During your season of weariness and wanting to let go of everything, you can't let go of your goals to complete and finish the course you have chosen and have been appointed to. The enemy's tactics never change in this world, he comes to kill, steal, and destroy. Don't fall into the plans of the enemy. Christ has already defeated him now we must remain powerful in retaining the win! How do we do this you ask? By staying steadfast and unmovable to the Lord with resistance against the enemy at all times.

The word of God tells us in 2 Thessalonians 3:13 and as for you brethren, do not become weary or lose heart in doing right but continue in well-doing without weakening. (Amplified Bible) We need people to speak into our lives with God intentions with wisdom revelation and instruction. Note this, information is good but you must apply the information to have a great outcome. You knowing something don't fix the problem or change the person. Using what you have does all that and more. We all need people to speak to us with the heart, mind, and council of God. Have people that can recognize your strengths and remind you of them to help you gain your focus on who you are and why you have come to a place and a people for a season. Choose people that love to build, and enjoy encouraging other people!

We declare that you will not grow weary in well doing without remembering who you are in Christ. We decree you shall build the people with encouragement and wealth of the Lord. We declare you will hold to the anointing of God and release over the people possibilities! You will enforce great manifestations of the Kingdom of God here! We declare you shall impart, stir, active, ignite, launch, challenge, and train the people to do the work, to create the plan, to follow the framework, to be refreshed and renewed daily. We declare you will train teams, build families, become involved in communities, develop strategies, equip ministers, aid and assist other pastors and churches by nurturing and developing them to grow and prosper. We declare you will invade territories occupy, overwhelm, and conquer with the power of possibilities of faith in Jesus Christ! We declare and decree you will succeed and become a model for others to follow in Jesus mighty name! We declare you will be a leader that will bring change to the minds of people that are stuck and drying up! We declare you shall establish healthy relationships as a leader and you will know the people and their strengths and you will launch and relaunch gifts, businesses, families, and people all around. We declare it so in the mighty name of Jesus Christ!

LEADING IN LOVE

If I can speak in the tongues of men and even angels, but have not love that reasoning, intentional, spiritual devotion such as is inspired by God's love for and in us, I am only a noisy gong or a clanging cymbal. I Corinthians 13:1 amplified bible.

Love is a powerful word to feel to use to express and to lead by. God operated in the act of love by giving the world His only son. Christ demonstrated the function of love as well as given us a blueprint of stewardship relationships and leadership. Strong's defines love, agape denotes an undefeatable benevolence and unconquerable goodwill that always seeks the highest goo of the other person, no matter what he does. It is the self-giving love that gives freely without asking anything in return, does not consider the worth of its object. Agape is more a love by choice than Phileo, which is love by chance; and it refers to the will rather than the emotion. Agape describes the unconditional love God has for the world. (Strong's definition).

Quote from Joel Manby: Agape love is the foundation for the best and noblest relationships that humans are capable of.

For leaders leading there must be a demonstration of agape love and this love is about behavior not emotion. When you look at the behavior and emotion position you must go to scripture for some instructions on loving and leading. Why would I even suggest doing so? How Christ led people to be healed was amazing. How Christ led people to be forgiven of sin is totally overwhelming. How Christ delivered people from demonic issues still mind blowing. Most of all how and why

Christ came to love us all we will never truly understand why. How Christ gave himself unselfishly even by his death.

I Corinthians 13:1-13 will take you step by step of how agape works. How agape love looks. How this love acts. How agape love looks on you. How this love holds up even under pressure. It goes on and on with so much inspiration to encourage a person about the possibilities of this unfailing love. It is important to learn to produce this behavior. This behavior is a successful leadership principle. When the attitude is altered then the behavior will change. Make it apart of your wardrobe inside and outside of you. Truly it is impossible to lead for Christ Jesus without this beautiful behavior agape love!

Leadership involves relationship. Loving well, listening well, speaking up well, correcting well, training well, behaving well, and trusting well. Leaders you will have to trust as well as becoming a trusted person yourself. Look at two things at one time Christ told the disciples to do. Love the Lord your God with all your heart, your soul, and your mind. And love your neighbor as you love yourself. When leading people as Christ lead His disciples, it will draw you into becoming accountable to the word and to your relationships. John 15: 10-17 the Lord speaks to His followers then as well as now. He talks to them about obeying the instructions of the commandments of loving Him is abiding in His love also. He also states that we love one another as He loves us. It amazes me how He reminds us that no one has greater love than His to where He laid down His life for a friend. Now that states that we are in a relationship with Him that is why He called us friend! Christ love shown even by His behavior to death and still after death on our behalf to still be available to us is absolutely beautiful to me. Now this is real love and real relationship, such powerful leadership to look upon and model. Jesus still speaks today for us to love each another not hate, mistreat, or abuse, but love as His has loved us all. I am bringing this behavior up for we must lead in agape love. Follow this and you will not fail God, the cause, the people, your relationships, or yourself.

Leaders we must examine if we are misusing the spiritual gifts of Christ. These gifts, sure they are without repentance but surely you must have a conscious about using them and standing in the name of the Lord God. Be careful of the conduct and behavior, it will have consequences to the outcome. We have agape love on the inside of us especially when functioning and operating in the spiritual gifts, imparting into the people, activating the people, empowering the people, training and developing the people, preaching and teaching the gospel of Christ, and the list goes on and on we must function and operate in agape love people of God! Stop getting caught up with ambition and you misunderstand the value of the anointing of Christ. Don't be misled by greed for power and money. All of your study and training will be no good for the people if you don't have love, love is the key! When we say we know Christ and abide in Christ our conduct is as the same as Christ. God perfects us and we completely reach maturity that's how we are recognized as being in Him. When we continue to walk in love we are saying we live by love we teach by love we preach by love and we lead by love guided by it and following it every day of our lives. Now this is one way people will know if you are the real deal or not. All they will need to do is check the fruit on your tree. If the tree is bearing a lot of fruit and love is one of the fruit, you are a true leader leading the way!

Love endures long and is patient and kind: love never is envious nor boils over with jealousy, is not boastful or vain glorious, does not display itself haughtily. It is not conceited arrogant and inflated with pride: it is not rude unmannerly and does not act unbecomingly. Love God's love in us does not insist on its own rights or its own way, for it is not self-seeking; it is not touchy or fretful or resentful; it takes no account of the evil done to it, it pays no attention to a suffered wrong. It does not rejoice at injustice and up righteousness, but rejoices when right and truth prevail. Love bears up under anything and everything that comes is ever ready to believe the best of every person, its hopes are fadeless under all circumstances, and it endures everything without weakening. I Corinthians 13:4-7 amplified bible.

We declare you will not fail because love never fades or fail. You shall overcome evil with good. You shall be a strong wall of defense against the devils schemes toward the body. You will lead healthy with people that are willing to be healthy. We decree that the power of love will flow from you in Jesus name. We decree the love behavior will arise among you and your team. We decree your teaching preaching instructing leading mentoring parenting and all forms of healthy relationships will be filled with love, the love the father has given and Christ has shown and taught. Be fruitful in this season and every season that you are in. Allow the fruit from your tree your field your baskets to flow, yield increase, to flood and feed. And with every chance you get release the power of love!

BUILDING RELATIONSHIPS

Being a leader leading you must learn to build relationships. When you learn to see people as the highest value, you will not wound them you will build them and impart value into their lives. Let's look at how Christ led. Christ built leaders to work and walk with Him. Christ ate with the leaders, He slept with the leaders, He traveled with the leaders, and He did the ministry with the leaders. Christ wanted them to see how, why and what He was doing. Having leaders being relational with the people is important. Building people up in their strengths, training them to lead in love, establishing skills and developing people to enjoy their family and life as well as enjoy leading, this is all in building relationships. I say having healthy relationships are vital for leadership". When people feel comfortable talking to you that shows a good sign of building. When people are able to express information about the team and the work of the team, you are building. What I am expressing is how you listen and talk with people you are training, is key in building and establishing relationship. Relationship expresses what it feels and look likes to be appreciated valued and loved. Leading as Christ, He was compassionate, loving, strong, powerful, understanding, loyal, conquering, and fulfilling. You will always need to model what you preach! Being a role to what you teach and instruct. Wear the fruit of Christ well and display pour out His greatest gift love! You will know if you are trusted or not, because you will see the investment. Give and it shall be given good measure press down and shaken together and running over will they pour into your bosom. For with the measure you deal out, with the measure you use when you confer benefits on others, it will be measured back to you. Luke 6:38 amplified bible. Be careful of speaking on how much you love God and live life by treating God's people with no respect, no honor, and no love. Your relationships with people will reflect how you value them and value yourself.

CONNECTING WITH PEOPLE

Unmet needs will cause us to become frustrated. Learn how to communicate with people in a healthy way. So what you are asking for want be misunderstood or even taken for granted. What happens when we are not understood or heard, we become upset and feel not valued and feel rejected. So our response to others shows defensive behavior and not a need to connect at all. Try communicating again with something you are asking for being attainable. This can lead to good conversation and or a disagreement. Why? People have a need to be needed, loved, valued, understood, and heard. We must understand that we are created to connect. Why build relationships? Because it shows connectivity to people, because we all want to be loved, heard, valued, understood, and appreciated. When you model who you are, it will draw many people to your sphere. By doing that, you must influence them with everything God has given you! Impact their lives with the gifts, the wisdom, and the grace you carry as a believer. We are all made in God's image and likeness. That is power and it is powerful! So we must show what God looks like in human form. We are a blueprint of His love. We are a framework of how He operates in relationship with us. We are literally His children here on earth. We are salt and light to this earth. We are growing and maturing with one another. We are His workmanship! If you are always talking and never listening, then it will be hard to have good communication. Leaders must be willing to hear what others are saying. This does not mean you have to agree but it does speak about your respect for the team of leaders you are pouring your heart into, leaders you are building for greatness, leaders that have and are being trained for commissioning! When a farmer spreads seed in the field the farmer is very mindful not to spread poison to kill the produce. Remember our words are like seeds planted in a field to yield good product they will raise up and speak what you have said. Trusting is showing maturity. Showing empathy is giving compassion. Understanding someone even when you don't agree delivers a sound communication skill. Know them that labor with you. Build your team strong.

CAREFUL MANAGEMENT

Take a few moments and look at your relationships. How are they? Are they loyal to you and vice versa? Do they value who you are? Do you value them? Do you communicate in any way?

We must learn to manage our relationships with care. Invest your time. Input your knowledge when needed. Always have understanding. Don't forget to check in on one another from time to time. Give your relationships a safe place to spill out issues of life. Let them know you are a safe place, and they can trust you with their heart. If people are seeking feedback in your conversation make sure you let them know what you want and what you are looking for from them. Just don't assume they know. Sometimes we can be so eager to share what's building in our brains. And we forget to share what's on our hearts. Remember sharing concerns will widen the intimacy with your relationships. Our emotions are connected to our soul and spirit and they are important and they do matter. When we are not a good fit in our relationships, learn where you do fit. We can be so quick and easy to give up on people because they don't fit our culture in Church, our culture in beliefs, our culture in religions and traditions. Stop trying to change people when you are building a relationship and team. Look at their strengths and value that. See where they can fit. Yes we are the body of Christ and we all do fit in the body of Christ. We should still be able to know who and where we can glean from without the other person feeling used or either feeling they are ahead of you as a leader. Proverbs speak about iron sharpening iron. This could be used as "I learn from you and you learn from me", but that does not always turn out that way. We must invest into our relationships with encouragement and love. Proverbs 16: 3 Amplified states, roll your works upon the Lord [commit and trust them wholly to Him; He will cause your thoughts to become agreeable to His will, and] so shall you plans be established and succeed. When we speak to one another we must remember our words are powerful. Your choice of handling problems or matters in life should not be forced by pressure from people. Leaders don't think that you are more important than the people you are pouring into. You must have a balance in all that you do as a leader. Knowing how far to go as in relationships. Your response to the people can be taken either seriously, controlling, demanding, and or it can be taken with love, care, consideration, and a healthy connection. Leaders to leaders are somewhat seemed as inner circle, looked at networks, alignments, and affiliates. Careful management in these areas of relationship can be overwhelming and a bit confusing. Requirements have become a little over the edge as far as connecting and building. Let's be transparent and totally free in our conversation on what we want from our relationships, and then we want have to be surprised and disappointed with how things turned out. Build on the good of one another and remember how we look to the world representing the body of Christ leading the way! Leaders we can do better building people to lead with us. One way I will express is, to become a story teller. Learn to tell your story. It gives and shows a place where you are vulnerable and transparent. So as you tell your stories some people will fill a need to share their stories too. As you listen to their stories you learn more about them. Things that are important to them and things that show their passion for what they believe. These are the things that are helpful and powerful towards connecting the ministers together. Sometimes using creativity will look like, reaching them with expressions of words appreciating them. While showing them how to share their experiences will help create a strong team of leaders. Knowing what each person brings to the team helps. Understanding each gift, strengths, and even their weakness will help build value to the team.

Webster's define the word builder like this, a person that builds or repairs things (such as houses, ships, bridges, etc.,) something that helps to develop or increase something. Building of character, development of position and operations are useful in project as well as only things. Here are two words that connect with builder, contractor (Overseer) and architect (designer, advisor, of the plans) these two have a strong role to operate and function in with building. If we would sometime think outside our mind how it normally functions we would like from our creative side of the brain and really become and operate with much innovation building the team to build the dream to empower building our relationships! Proverbs 14:1 amplified bible says, every wise woman builds her house, but the foolish one tears it down with her own hands. Can you imagine in this scripture her hands define her behavior or her own actions? If we are not careful maintaining our relationships with a good behavior we will tear down our houses (relationships) our structures we have built. We must use words that will build up and not tear down. Now it is true there may come a time that you will need to repair what has been torn down, and even in the repairing stage we must be wise master builders especially using the team to help do the work. 1 Corinthians 3:9-10 amplified bible says, for we are fellow workman (joint promoter, labors together) with and for God; you are God's garden and vineyard and field under cultivation, [you are] God's building. According to the grace (the special endowment for my task) of God bestowed on me, like a skillful architect and master builder I laid [the] foundation, and now another [man] is building upon it. But let each [man] be careful how he builds upon it. When we as leaders remember who created all of us foundational masterpieces of God, then maybe we will treat our relationships with grace and value the builder and building.

Ricky and I had to go through some crazy struggles pastoring. Why? Because we just assumed everybody was thinking the same as us. Pastors I know you probably can witness to that, especially when you are first starting out. However learning people and church systems and then learning how to trust and rely on Holy Spirit, you better know we learned some stuff! Pastoring was a great experience for both of us. Ricky and I would not have had the experiences, development, training, the blessings, the storms, and places to go if we did not have the people to pastor, lead, train, build, love, learn, make mistakes, and mature. The people helped process and develop who we are today. We made trademarks and built powerful relationships with the leaders we lead and ministers we trained and people we pastored and truly valued. This journey has been awesome, crazy, painful, but yet so inspiring. We had to let somethings go that God didn't need! Yes, it is true you will carry things around with you that God doesn't need. Then we started building and cultivating people and the reason to get them from place of thinking to living as believing. My husband and I were being built for something more than church effects, church programs, annual days, youth days, and so much more. That's when we changed how we listened and heard the spirit of the Lord lead and guide us another way. We enjoyed connecting with people and building relationships. Relationships they are a key to modeling the body of Christ and the kingdom. I just want to leave this chapter by saying this, "relationships do matter"!

We declare that people who call on the name of Jesus connect themselves to one another as the body to represent the body to be the whole message of the body of Christ. We declare a strong hunger to build relationships healthy relationships to symbolize our Father is not short of His promises to us all. Creating a culture of the Kingdom of Heaven in the earth, shows the King being present inside us with full demonstration of His love and power released from us. We release the power of the word of God to come alive in us all. Truly representing who we are in Christ, why we are created to live, to breathe, move, and have our being. Now Father we thank you that Christ prayed that we be one as you and Him are one. Let your grace be a seal over our lives forever, amen.

believe we have lost the true reason and left the compass to lead and guide us the right way. We must return to the right way with no dispute! Holy Spirit is left here for us all purposely to aid and assist all the way if we allow him to do what he was left to do, keep us aligned with Christ and heaven. Yes will have different things to do but yes we must not allow them to be greater than the love God gave us for each other. The love and unity Christ prayed for us to be one. We are a force to come against with no power to defeat us when we come together as we are made to. We are fighting each other and I am sure we are a little over worked at that battle. We are not made to fight each other we were made created saved baptized filled the Holy Spirit and release with power from on high also let's not forget forgiven and blessed beyond measure to be a powerful unit of oneness of Christ here in the earth modeling the King and His Kingdom!

I want to share the book of 1 Corinthians chapter 12 amplified bible. Now about the spiritual gifts the (special endowments of supernatural energy), brethren, I do not, want you to be misinformed. You know that when you were heathen, you were led off after idols that could not speak [habitually] as impulse directed and whenever the occasion might arise. Therefore I want you to understand that no one speaking under the power and influence of the [Holy] Spirit of God can [ever] say, Jesus is [my] Lord, except by and under the power and influence of the

Holy Spirit. Now there are distinctive varieties and distributions of endowments (gifts, extraordinary powers distinguishing certain Christians, due to the power of divine grace operating in their souls by the Holy Spirit) and they vary, but the [Holy] Spirit remains the same. And there are distinctive varieties of service and ministration, but it is the same Lord [Who is served]. And there are distinctive varieties of operation [of working to accomplish things], but it is the same God Who inspires and energizes them all in all. But to each one is given the manifestation of the [Holy] Spirit [the evidence, the spiritual illumination of the Spirit] for good and profit. To one is given in and through the [Holy] Spirit [the power to speak] a message of wisdom, and to another [the power to express] a word of knowledge and understanding according to the same [Holy] Spirit; to another [wonder-working] faith by the same [Holy] Spirit, to another the extraordinary powers of healing by the one Spirit; to another the working of miracles, to another prophetic insight (the gift of interpreting the divine will and purpose); to another the ability to discern and distinguishing between [the utterances of true] spirits [and false ones], to another various kinds of [unknown] tongues, to another the ability to interpret [such] tongues. All these [gifts, achievements, abilities] are inspired and brought to pass by one and the same [Holy] Spirit, Who apportions to each person individually [exactly] as He chooses. For just as the body is a unity and yet has many parts, and all the parts, though many, form [only] one body, so it is with Christ (the Messiah, the Anointed One). For by [means of the personal agency of] one [Holy] Spirit we were all, whether Jews or Greeks, slaves or free, baptized [and by baptism united together] into one body, and all made to drink of one [Holy] Spirit. For the body does not consist of one limb or organ but of many. If the foot should say, because I am not the hand, I do not belong to the body, would it be therefore not [a part] of the body? If the ear should say, because I am not the eye, I do not belong to the body, would it be therefore no [a part] of the body? If the whole body were an eye, where [would be the sense of] hearing? If the whole body were an ear, where [would be the sense of] smell? But as it is, God has placed and arranged the limbs and organs in the body, each [particular one] of them, just as He wished and saw fit and with the best adaptation. But if [the whole] were all a single organ, where would the body be? And now there are [certainly] many limbs and organs, but a single body. And the eye is not able to say to the hand, I have no need of you, nor again the head to the feet, I have no need of you. But instead there is [absolute] necessity for the parts of the body that are considered the more weak. And those [parts] of the body which we consider rather ignoble are [the very parts] which we invest with additional honor, and our unseemly parts and those unsuitable for exposure are treated with seemliness (modesty and decorum), which our more presentable parts do not require. But God has so adjusted (mingled, harmonized, and subtly proportioned the parts of) the whole body, giving the greater honor and richer endowment to the inferior parts which lack [apparent importance], So that there should be no division or discord or lack of adaptation [of the parts of the body to each other], but the members all alike should have a mutual interest in and care for one another. And if one member suffers, all the parts [share] the suffering; if one member is honored, all the members [share in] the enjoyment of it. Now you [collectively] are Christ's body and [individually] you are members of it, each part severally and distinct [each with his own place and function]. So God has appointed some in the church [for His own use]: first apostles (special messenger); second prophets (inspired preachers and expounders); third teachers; then wonder-workers; then those with ability to heal the sick; helpers; administrators; [speakers in] different (unknown) tongues. Are all apostles (special messengers)? Are all prophets (inspired interpreters of the will and purposes of God)? Are all teachers? Do all have the power of performing miracles? Do all possess extraordinary powers of healing? Do all speak with tongues? Do all interpret? But earnestly desire and zealously cultivate the greatest and the best gifts and graces (the higher gifts and the choicest graces). And yet I will show you a still more excellent way [one that is better by far and the highest of them all------love].

I believe so deep in my being that chapter 12 verses 1-31 has given us all a blueprint, a plan, a guide, and a measuring line to help us know and even remember who we are in the body. Who we are to each other and what we are to do. But truly having gifts does us no good or the people any good without the greatest gift. We need to pick the gift of love up and use it well and let it be found faithful inside us functioning to the full works it is created to do! Being different does speak a lot about the body of Christ. Being diverse, and particular, peculiar, infinite sequence and distinguishable as you and as the body of Christ. I enjoy this mix this varied and various distinctive parts we all bring to show forth the power of the King and His kingdom! We should look and observe our operations and functions and value, build, uphold, communicate, help, aid, assist, share, and love each other the more. Seeing that we matter to the Father, to Christ, to Holy Spirit, we would at least matter to one another as well.

LEADERS BEING BUILT FOR SOMETHING

I love the story of Joseph how he was chosen of his father to lead the way. Even though Joseph's brothers did not agree due to the fact that he was not the oldest or in their sight qualified. But here is my point. Joseph was satisfied with just being trained to lead sheep, goats, whatever flock they had, but leading a portion of things in a desert, he just wanted to obey and please his father. However, the brothers got crazy with jealousy and became over taken with envy and strife. With that said it led to Joseph's departure into slavery. While in bondage he still prayed to God believing something would happen as he prayed, I know we can all agree with that because we feel that same way at times of praying especially during crisis situations. Joseph brought abundance to the house, the staff, and the land he was enslaved to. Suddenly something else changed to Joseph he was lied on and sent away to prison again. Now he was in Pharaoh's prison as seen as a man not worthy to live. How I visit this next divine appointment is like this. Pharaoh had a dream that no one in his courts or no one on his team could interpret the dream. God is so awesome when He sets up divine appointments no one can interfere with who he has planned to do the work. So someone tells Pharaoh of a man who can interpret dreams, and Pharaoh sends for him and that man is Joseph. Now if Joseph had not gone to interpret the dreams of Pharaoh the world system would not have been able to crossover into the plan God had prepared for Joseph. The people would not have been able to endure a crisis time of hardness. The people would not have known what to do with what they had to make it multiply and bring great abundance during their time of great supply. All that Joseph had been through, it was a process and development in the making of a leader in an economy where no one could image grace would be there for them. Joseph was being built for leadership not to his culture of people but to all in that area and region. He was prepared for something greater than what he could see in the desert. He was taken shaken and moved from what was familiar to him. Faith was working all around him without him even knowing what was ahead. Just note it took some years! So don't quit, don't fall away, don't disappear, and stop complaining. God is building you for something greater you can't see it yet. I know you dream and see all sorts of things in the spirit realm that comes to pass but this right here what God is doing you can't see it but it is sure to come to you. What God has planned is for a people, a region, a culture, a nation that will need a leader that will bring change and so much more from the Lord. You have been going through much suffering and hell. Being held up, jacked up, talked about, misunderstood, persecuted and lied on. You are being processed and developed for something far beyond your thinking now. You have been purposed for something greater than you. Your divine appointment will be something different than you preaching in a conference or preaching at a church service. Whatever it is God's got it especially for you and it is nothing no one can do to stop or block what He has prepared. Leaders all over the world not leaders you see operating large and out front. I am talking about people that have been in bondage in prison, overlooked, lied upon, cheated out of position; I'm talking about the people that are not looking to be placed up. God got them and He is building and developing them for what He wants to happen in our world. Let's get excited something and some people are about to break forth and interpret the dreams of the future. People don't miss this move of God.

My statement "I WAS MADE FOR THIS"!

Different leaders look like this, Builders, Bridges, Motivators, Innovators, Life Coaches, Mentors, Trainers, Connectors, Strategist, Pioneers, Forerunners, Pastors, Teachers, Apostles, Prophets, Evangelist, and there are more. We must keep empowering others and one another. We need to stay connected with some form of communication. We should continue to build each other and keep the persons strengths before them in a way of respect and honor to allow humbling to grow gracefully. All of our gifts heave a momentum in them to move and we must keep movement mobilizing others. This is one fact of team building. We are all one the same team and team members help each other. Being made up of different things will cause us to be stronger mightier and powerful in all we will do. Having a positive outlook at who we are helps us keep unity alive and vibrant. Leaders we must learn to access the perceptions of the team the body of Christ and even the team you build. Create a safe place for your team during your training and equipping. So when mistakes happen they will still feel valued and accepted. We will miss somethings and not have it right or fitted, but the joy is knowing you have built relationships with the people and they understand your heart and you understand their heart. Creating that safe place to learn is really important. Leaders remember we need people around you to mirror and reflect how you lead. That will keep a healthy balance in your evaluation of self and of your team. Their is something that you need to understand, the people you will build, train, equip, develop, and have a relationship with they must be commissioned out to do the work. Staying under you, staying in the building with you does not prove you are a great leader or prove that this is God's way. Leaders, plant those seeds (leaders) plant those trees (leaders) and help them grow!

A LEADERS LEADER

All through the New Testament scriptures of the apostles and their works, they went out by two to do the work traveling all over. You must have people you trust with your emotions. You need people to hear your heart and decisions to make choices.

Hear you when you need empathy or just to keep you aligned to Holy Spirit at all times. These are just a few things to share I am sure you can come up with some great ideas as well to share with others. Remember having a leader or leaders speak in your life should not represent slavery! Dictating things to you, asking you to pay the toll before the conversation (their time is valuable sow money) and showing much control over your life. Know and understand the relationship of having this in your life. Be clear on it, discuss it, and pray about what you need and what you can offer in return if needed. Really this is relationship and this is what we can make available for each other. What you do for others may not be spoken of until you feel like you are out of everything. Keep doing what you do for your relationships. You may be the encourager and that is a strength skill of your personality so encourage and keep it moving. You may have much compassion for your relationships to where you are always available when they need you for prayer or understanding. This could be your strength skill, use it and keep it moving. Just keep doing what you do it, it works. Don't look for that skill set to always come back to you from the people you gave to, these things will return to you and will bless you as you have blessed others. Be the Body of Christ. 1 Corinthians 1:7 that you come short in no gift related to other words derived from Charisma. It shows joy, cheerfulness, delight, grace, goodwill, undeserved favor, a free gift, divine gratuity, spiritual endowment, miraculous faculty. These are available to all in the Body of Christ representing the power of Christ.

TRAINING LEADERS TO LEAD

The definition of train is to, cause to acquire knowledge or skill in some field. I remember when we decided to train the ministers in deliverance. This subject was different for everyone and new to some of them, and Ricky and I had already been studying and had some rather close up experiences with it. So as we began the training session everyone had their own booklet and bible. As the teaching started I noticed some clearing of throats and coughing. The tension started building in the room and all at once, a loud noise came from a person at the end of the table and demonic manifestation broke out like a bad rash, it was all over the room! Oh boy! I was ready and excited about getting the people free from strongholds and unclean spirits! Even though my husband and I were first-timers, we refuse to give up until freedom was obtained. Finally, everyone ministered freedom, love, and restoration with such a passion of victory of Christ! This true story is just the example of teaching ministers to lead. Being set free will allow you to free others with grace of the Father. Training ministers how to deliver God's people is what Christ did with His disciples. We desired to teach and instruct ministry work different from what they already knew and some that did not know at all. Instructing a new learning behavior will be challenging but keep teaching in order to create a new habit. In coaching them in group sessions we would stay focused on asking them to stay focused on renewing their mind to the mind of Christ. This is a practice that must be done daily renewal it helps to build the new behavior and create a new pattern. The word of God states, therefore if any person who is in grafted in Christ the Messiah he is a new creation a new creature altogether; the old previous moral and spiritual condition has passed away. Behold the fresh and new has come! (Amplified bible)

Teaching leaders to be adaptive in their training will be testing limits in a person's mind-set to how things should go or how things should be. You know the old saying, "if it isn't broke don't bother it", or "we been doing things this way for years". My husband and I have discovered training leaders with an adaptive attitude causes leaders to focus on people knowing how to change when change comes. Knowing what that looks like, and how to feel when making that decision. Many great leaders in history books most of them encountered changing environments, changing behaviors, changing atmospheres, and changing the way you treat people as a leader. 1 Corinthians 2:4-7 says, and my language and my message were not set forth in persuasive (enticing and plausible) words of wisdom, but they were in demonstration of the [Holy] Spirit and power [a proof by the Spirit and power of God, operating on me and stirring in the minds, of my hearers the most holy emotions and thus persuading them], so that your faith might not rest in the wisdom of men (human philosophy), but in the power of God. Yet when we are among the full-grown (spiritually mature Christians who are ripe in understanding), we do impart a [higher] wisdom (the knowledge of the divine plan previously hidden); but it is indeed not a wisdom of this present age or of this world nor of the leaders and rulers of this age, who are being brought to nothing and are doomed to pass away. But rather what we are setting forth is a wisdom of God once hidden [from human understanding] and now revealed to us by God—[that wisdom] which God devised and decreed before the ages for our glorification [to lift us into the glory of His presence]. We must come to understand how we should do things with wisdom of God. Looking at the scriptures helped us to see adaptive leadership is about how leaders encourage people to adapt to problems, understand transitions, work on transformation, see reformation as leading, being sensitive to change and how to shift from one paradigm to the next, empowered with God's power to transform cultures and regions. Adaptive leadership focuses on the adaptations required of people in response to changing environments. We prepare and encourage people to deal with change. Remember going through, your thrust is greater in what you are doing than the opposition that is attacking and opposing you. Some of us right now are a part of someone's transformation. Leaders help other leaders lead the way.

LEADERS IMPACTING LEADERS

The word impact is defined as, to have a direct effect or impact on something or someone. This word also states to effect, impress, influence, move, reach, and to touch.

Investing in a person's life will bring impact to them. How does that work? When you show people that you are modeling how to live this life of Christ you normally do what Christ says to do! Yep, that was easy. So as we go about being all that the Lord has created and declared we are, we show a model of leading. That model gives a beautiful plan of effective leadership. In order to lead you need to know how to follow, that's why I said, modeling what Christ left for us to do will be and become effective in the people that you lead. Yes, it does impress others. And that impressive behavior creates fruit that is connected to the true vine, Jesus Christ! When your behavior produces how you live, then people you train will have a view of accountability and integrity coming from you leading the way! I remember a time in service and I was literally called out by someone speaking their ideal of what they thought they knew about me. The person asked to have a word and she was allowed. So as she began to tell me off with how I need to preach different and stop preaching about leaving sin and start preaching what people need to hear then we would have more people to join the church! When I heard that I stepped out and my husband grabbed my skirt! I looked at him and said what! He told me look at the enemy calling you out to fight in your flesh to bring shame to you with everyone watching? How can you fix that when the damage is done! Boy I was heated and ready to take her out! Then the spirit of the Lord said, not by might but by my spirit! So I walked over to the mic, looked at the congregation, some of the people stood up and was ready for me to say, "get her" or ready to hear me say, "the devil is a liar", but instead I just preached the word of God in love with full passion ignited up to the totally degree! I left no room for the enemy to win nowhere and as I preached, prayed, and ministered love at the altar to all, even the lady that blasted me I loved on her with no resentment at all. I rejoiced so much so till I was full with expectation of the Holy Spirit to fall on us all! Waiting for more maturity to rise inside me, more accountability to be seen of me, more integrity to be lifted up and out from me. Yes! That was a day of transformation for me!

I came from a place of its not about me it's about living this life for Christ! I reached more people that day with the message of Christ all because I was challenged to change my ways of reacting to someone's opinion about me in Christianity.

Don't allow your personal trials and storms become hurtful to others. I said that with this thought, many leaders have spoken to others they train telling them, "you didn't suffer like I suffered".

Or saying, "this anointing is too costly for me to impart to others that didn't go through like I did"! Those training guides are not helpful to building and developing leaders. I get it we all didn't suffer like Christ did. We all didn't pay the price He did. We were not rejected and bruised like He was. But it didn't and has not and will not stop Him from releasing His anointing upon all our lives! Praise you Jesus for choosing to give us all that we need to minister your gospel! Think about it, we must be willing as a believer of the gospel of Christ by sowing into others with love and impartations of things that benefit the body of Christ. Think about how powerfully effective that will be. Leaders are not in demand for telling people what to do; they are in demand for showing people how to do it!

Just because you are not pastoring a people or maybe you are not leading a group in a church. This does not mean you cannot lead and you are not a leader!

BECOMING A STRONG STRUCTURE

I was driving across the bridge one day. As I looked at the vehicles I was amazed at how we simply trust the structure of a bridge. I just began to thank God for crossing over; I don't even know why I prayed that prayer at the moment. But when I finished I heard the spirit of the Lord say to me, "you are in a place of crossing over. You are going from one place to the next"! I declared what I heard with such excitement in my pitch and tone! As I arrived home I said, "I'm just like a bridge". I looked the word up and I just laughed so loud, and I began confessing that I was a strong safe structure for people to crossover into life, in anything they were dealing with, and whatever they hoped to do. So I wrote how this was important as a type of symbol to leaders in the church and just leaders everywhere. Stated, in every transitional period or season in the earth God places leaders to be as bridges for others to cross over. I realized doing this moment, transition was never going to leave our life and we had an opportunity to be involved in transition or never realize it is something we will all go through, experience, and be a part or not in life. So why would I use the word bridge as a building and training tool for leaders? I believe we will always need strong reliable structures for crossover. For crossover is a place of transitional establishment. Ricky and I just decided that we would train, teach, guide, help, and assist leaders in their transitional periods. These periods or seasons can feel so lonely or seem so far away in the distance, like unable to reach.

But how easy is it for you as a leader to assume that a hard time or a transitional period will not be a pathway for generations to learn from and be built by. I can go on and on, but the idea is this. You must remain teachable so you can develop process and learn all that the Spirit of the Lord is bring to you for leading the way.

Holy Spirit, we declare that the leaders that are leading will have and keep a teachable spirit. We declare strength to the leaders now in Jesus name! Be transitional and be ready at all times when you speak and move us in difficult places, disturbing situations, and hard painful times. We release a strong endurance upon your leaders. We release creativity to speak and build momentum. We call forth supernatural angelic assistance to be with us helping us come into advancing as the leader you spoke us to become. We declare the worth and power of who you are Jesus. Show yourself strong and be great to us now and forever more, Amen!

CHALLENGES OF A LEADER

Ricky and I have had some challenging times in ministry. Operating and functioning in the gifts, the positions, building leadership teams, training ministers, pastoring, and of course being married with a family. It was different and difficult understanding or trying to understand transition, seasons of change, faith to faith when we thought the faith we had was fine, the time of waiting, being sensitive to the voice of Holy Spirit more than to the pain of our crisis! Yes there are and will be challenging times. I believe that it may not be or have been a lot of discussion on challenges of a leader. Some people have thought it might be too personal or it would cause misunderstanding. However we as leaders have a team of people trained to minister to the needs of leaders. Or maybe if you don't listen to the spirit of the Lord speak to you to choose which way to go or what choice to make, then you could escape that challenge! So true, it is a choice to make and a risk to take for many. But, we have learned and found out being in Christ trusting Him, operating in faith, just literally taking a jump into knowing more about Him, it is risky. But life is all about risks and learning what to do and what not to do. That is why we cannot stop this path we have chosen with Christ to become expanded, built, upgraded, pushed into faith more, and the list could keep going on and on. So, without failures in things of our life we would not have a personal experience. If we did not have test and trial in leading, ministering, then you would not have a personal experience with hearing Christ speak to you by Holy Spirit in your crisis times or just anytime in your life. Just on that note, we would like to discuss and share this. It seemed at this time in our life Holy Spirit was just asking us for too much to give. I just wanted to disappear. Even saying that, I had such a hunger inside of me fighting to awake and live greater! Ricky was placed in a time of seeking the Lord so strong to the point I had to remind him he was a parent, husband and he had other things he needed to do. I know, it is so funny talking about it but yet it is so true. When you want more of God you must be aware that you need to build your relationship with the Lord and know so personally for yourself when you hear Him speak through Holy Spirit relating things of His heart to you.

BEING SENSITIVE TO CHANGE

Developing a listening ear to hear what is being said to you by Holy Spirit.   Hearing the simple things in life without complaining about why the spirit of the Lord is speaking to me about what He wants said, done, achieved ministered released and when it will take place.   I didn't say you couldn't ask, I just said don't complain when you hear and see what the spirit of the Lord is speaking to you about you or God's people. Training your personal nature not to be in charge but allowing your spirit man guided by Holy Spirit to show you the way, tell you when, release to you the cause and effect of the matter, telling or showing you where, and of course building your faith to do what has been requested to do. The sensitivity is important for the reasons of your motives are not always personal and always first. Knowing exactly what has been released to you is for a people in a city or a people in the church, or a family group, a business project, the success of a people, a nation, or a culture needing upgrade, a religion, or maybe you. I have a story about releasing prophecy. I heard and saw what the Lord had showed me and spoke to me. I listened to see if it was for that time or another time. And I just felt a release to deliver the word. Words released are so time sensitive in the natural and the supernatural and it's hard for people to acknowledge that importance. So I ministered the prophetic words, gave spiritual insight to the word, and also encourage the person to trust Holy Spirit right at that time so they could receive of the Lord. I felt fear grab the person but I knew the person really needed this word along with direction and instructions of how to. So when the person wouldn't come forth I just prayed on their behalf. So church was over and I knew the person would come to me afterward. When that happened I did not go hard on them I encourage them not to let a time go by when the spirit of the Lord was pouring out just what that person had been praying for. With that said, I let the person know the value of knowing their God His Son and Holy Spirit was so powerful in a person's life. I released the word gave directions and instructions not with anger because they didn't come forth earlier but with love and correction with an understanding of how Christ loves us all and timing and being sensitive to time is important because it always lead us to how to do it, which way, and a certainty of when. Trusting Holy Spirit is so key as a believer and a great powerful door of opportunity could be right before you, but if you have no spiritual awareness to what is happening around you or in the moment you could miss it.

There were many times the Lord spoke for us to shift, for us to change the way we praised and worship, to transition from one level of praying to another and continuing, our faith raising up from last year's faith to building momentum and mobilizing our faith. We had come to a point it was so much to learn and model all we had received during our times of fasting and praying.   The giving model, the helping model, the receiving model, the pioneer model, forerunner model, builder model, and so much more. These times were so crucial to us, to others, and to our region. Leaders must know when it's time to transition from one point to the next.

Philippians 2:13-14 Not in your own strength for it is God who is all the while effectually at work in you energizing and creating in you the power and desire, both to will and to work for His good pleasure and satisfaction and delight. Do all things without grumbling and faultfinding and complaining against God and questioning and doubting among yourselves. Instead of complaining start creating! Don't speak negative of the problems you have or the test you are going through. Stop believing the lie the enemy has told you! You have power to speak to the circumstance and cause a change to happen. You are not bound to the word of the enemy you are bound to the word of God. Listen to Holy Spirit tell you to engage in battle, to renew your mind daily, to fill your life up again, to be empowered again and again. Raise that banner high above your name. Be bold and courageous in the Lord. Believe that He that has begun the work in you will not stop until He has completed it. You are a work of Christ and the builder will not stop filling you up with Himself until all the work is complete here and now. I know you may have thought about giving up, stopping, or no longer useful to stand, guess what you and probably a whole lot more have gone through that moment. Be sensitive to why God has called you. Be more sensitive to He saved you and delivered you to save and deliver His people. Acts chapter 14:22 says, establishing and strengthening the souls and the hearts of the disciples, urging and warning and encouraging them to stand firm in the faith, and telling them that it is through many hardships and tribulations we must enter the kingdom of God. We never thought we would have to go through tribulation, suffering, brokenness, or anything that would take much effort in work. We thought accepting Jesus Christ speaking in tongues and being filled with Holy Spirit would stop that from happening, not! So through our experiences of growing pains and learning to know God and build a relationship with the Lord it has been good. Process for development provides good experience. As we evolve in the world by time in seasons through experience even of our faint. Will we stand limited in our thinking or will we walk into our possibilities. When you think powerful you will reflect powerful you will reflect who created you. When you reflect encouragement to others build their weakness and keep building them stronger.   This is how you know to show and share all God has shown and shared with you. We must show these things and many other things to others and each other for it is all about relating with one another building relationships with one another it really reflects how the Lord waits to speak and communicate with us all. Ricky and I believe leaders have a power to empower people not enslave people. Spiritual authority is not abusive and enslavement. It builds leads impact imparts develops creates innovates and fosters love in a healthy respectful way. It nurtures and cultivates not destroy those who are of the body of Christ. Building leaders to lead the way is not about your personal gain or agenda. It is about the handiwork of Christ the framework of Christ being lived and enjoyed. It is not all about how well you can preach, teach, instruct, lead, administrate, prophesy, evangelize, train, facilitate conferences, or even have churches submit to your leadership. But truly I tell you it is about how well you model them all by the life you love and live.

When we learn to see people as valuable and understand and know how to share that with them, we will be reflecting what Christ did. This journey is about experiencing the development of living out," in Christ I live I move and I have my being"! Being in Christ and Christ being in you!

There is always so much more we could write. But we hope you grab the baton and run with it even greater. Your experiences with the Lord are needed and valued. Sharing them would bless, help, and assist many.

THOUGHTS FOR ENCOURAGEMENT

- Building leadership is empowering people to innovate and create.
- Leaders change a status, a moment, an environment, a life, a relationship, and a generation.
- Your pain and suffering does not identify you. Stop complaining and start creating.
- Build a habit of discovering your strengths to focus your life on not only your weaknesses.
- Be mindful of the messages you speak to yourself and others daily.

- Building bridges for crossover are more successful than digging ditches for someone to fall.

- No one can use you, but when you give of yourself is grace showing goodwill.
- Leaders develop a strategy to connect the gap between generations.
- Leaders are like planes, trains, automobiles, and Buses; they transport people from one place of thinking to the next.
- Leaders light up dark pathways during times of crisis and storms.
- Leaders are like generators, they give power and are resourceful always.
- Leaders are like a good chiropractor they know how to make the right alignment in the body.

ENDORSEMENTS

Ricky and D'Andrea helped me to overcome every obstacle standing in my way. As a wounded young pastor, they loved me back to life and showed me that I could trust again. They encouraged me to be the best in God that I could be. They mentored me in the Apostolic and Prophetic and pushed me to my destiny. They taught in word but more importantly they modeled it for me. Today, I know the Thomas' as Kingdom Builders who love the Body of Christ. Their specialty is building people through building relationships. Their love for God is shown through their love for God's people, no strings attached. The strong Apostolic and Prophetic release through their ministries is God's seal of them in the earth realm. They are true Apostles who exhibit self-less acts while working to help people rise from the ashes to become powerful forces that will leave legacies for generations to come. I am truly grateful for the ministry of God that lies within them. I have experienced the impact that their ministry brings to individuals and as well as to regions. These leaders have modeled the way for me and many others before me and after me. Without such great mentors, many of us would not be correctly demonstrating God's Kingdom in the earth. Ricky and D'Andrea Thomas truly are Leaders Leading The Way!

Apostle Stephanie Palmer
Kingdom Builders Church International
Stephanie Palmer Ministries

The Apostle Paul says, I am made all things to all men, that I night by all means save some. I have just described Ricky and D'Andrea Thomas. I have known them for more than 10 years and they have been great friends to me and our church family. When I needed a friend in the ministry to talk, counsel, correct, instruct, teach, preach or prophesy with love and precision in the spirit. I would call and they would deliver just what the spirit of God said. We consider family, strength and honor. Ricky and D'Andrea are great friends to us.

Apostle Glen Evans
Redeemed Christian Center
Bradenton, Fl.

I had the privilege of meeting Apostle Ricky and Prophet D'Andrea Thomas 8years ago. They have really impacted my life concerning ministry, communication and sharing practical life skills that are connected with the word of God. God is really using them to impart revelation, wisdom, and kingdom truths concerning covenant relationships to the body of Christ. They are a true apostolic father and mother to so many bringing transformation and restoration to marriages and covenant relationships within the body of Christ I believe this book is a must read for believers and all mankind from any ethnical background.

Apostle Kevin Bailey
Touch of the Master Healing Ministries International

There are people in the world that are transformers, with a loving and genuine spirit, and committed to helping others become the best they can be. In our lives, those people are Ricky and D'Andrea Thomas. We were blessed to be a part of their ministry for over 14 years in Oklahoma City, Ok. As visionary leaders they demonstrated the importance of growing a team, serving with humility, and honoring the voice of God in everything you do in ministry. As leaders they always led their members to make a choice in their belief and knowledge of God. The door was always left open to ask questions, discover together, and learn from every lesson that life presented. Their work was Christ's work of the ministry of reconciliation. As a minister they were our "spiritual echo in our lives", always speaking our heart for God, and never in judgement. We began as ministry companions, and grew into leaders, and now we call them friends and family. Through their acceptance of us at critical moments in our life we were able to see beyond our own pain to minister to others. It is with honor, we share this acknowledgement of their servant leadership in the ministry and the impact on our lives, family, and ministry. Ricky and D'Andrea thank you for your compassionate leadership, authenticity, and for sharing in Sunday fellowship dinner every week. We love you and you're an integral part of the family we have become.

Webster~Kelly~Jason~Jeremiah
The Ramsey's
Without you there would be no us

In my 32 years of ministry and 20 plus years as a Pastor and leader, I have been so blessed by God to have Ricky and D'Andrea Thomas as my Spiritual Leaders and Mentors. The insight and wisdom that they have gleaned over the years and shared Is phenomenal. They have been so unselfish to pass to the next generation of leaders and share them with The Kingdom of God as we'll as The Marketplace.

Apostle Shelia Jefferson
President and Co-Founder Soul Harbor Outreach

Giving thanks to God for this opportunity to introduce my experience with you. Truly it's an honor to express the heart felt impact you made in my life. God used you both tremendously in many ways of my maturity and growth in Him. The training, equipping, and imparting by way of teaching the word, traveling as a team, and personal time together has helped me flourish into the woman of God I am today. Words on paper could never thank you enough for the countless prayers, prophecy, and encouraging words, you spoke over my life. I am grateful to have had you come into my life because of the life lessons learned in my growing. They are a great asset to any individual who wants to make a change in their life for the Kingdom of Heaven.

Prophetess Eloise G. Dixon CPC, CYPFC, CAC

For those of you who do not know these two powerhouses of God. You will see God manifested power demonstrating in them through the word with fire and power. God had given us a treasure unto the body of Christ, to help compel and mature the body into its God given rightful place. God has placed a mighty mandate on them to help bring leaders, lay persons and the body into a place of who they are and how to walk into their God given rights. Being connected to their ministry since 2002 has helped thrust us to who we always knew we would be. Their leading and guidance took us to another level. Now, we impart to the church as we have been taught to pursue the true foundation of the Cornerstone Church.

Apostle Mario and Joyce Lopez
New Covenant Christian Servicemen Center
Seoul, Korea

We have known both Apostles Ricky and D'Andrea Thomas for over 10 years and recognize them as great prophetic ministers to the Body of

Christ. Apostle Ricky and D'Andrea have a commitment to helping people through focusing on building the body of Christ. They are trail blazers, reformers, and indispensable resource to the Body of Christ and doctrinally reliable. Apostles Ricky and D'Andrea skillful gifting's and Godly insights advance the Body of Christ and are a blessing to those who encounter them. We acknowledge and recognize Apostles Ricky and D'Andrea Thomas as great gifts to and for the Body of Christ.

Pastors Michael and Claretta Woods
Heavenly Smiles Outreach Ministry
Midwest City, Ok

Many writers take on the topic of leadership without the history and practical experience to go with it. For Prophet D'Andrea Thomas and Apostle Ricky Thomas, this is not the case. They have a proven record of tested leadership experience. From an early age, prophet Thomas showed that the anointing of the Lord was evident in her life. In addition, that anointing made room for her at every stage of her development. From her start as an organist/worship leader to founding a ministry that networked with other leaders around the nation and world, Prophet Thomas has established herself as a pioneer and spiritual administrator. Leadership as defined by Merriam-Webster is having the capacity to lead. Her capacity has not just been with words, but with evidence of other leaders birthed and lives changed through her ministry. I count it an honor to endorse her work and recommend her as well versed voice on the topic of leadership.

Apostle J.C. Bradley LPC, Ph.D-ABD
Pastor of Higher Purpose Christian Center International

I truly admire this loving and connected couple. D'Andrea and Ricky Thomas expose their lives to all who are in need of redirection. Having worked closely with D'Andrea and Ricky changing couples outlook to a healthy and non-threatening relationship, I found trust at the core of winning connections. This couple has met the challenge by building trust in their relationships and connections, causing everyone in the vicinity to thrive.

Jacquelyn R. Hatcher Masters Mental Health Counselor PhD candidate

D'Andrea is a prophetess that has the ability to release wisdom, revelation, and activation into leaders. She has an ability to see the unseen and bring it into the visible room so that we can produce fruit on a level that is unprecedented. With a natural gift of encouragement with wisdom and experience along with the ability to apply the word of God to business, church, and family this woman bring to the table a now word for people in leadership roles. If you are a leader this is a book that you will want to read because she will encourage you, she will correct you, and she will cause you to step into your destiny on the level you could not have done on your own. I highly recommend this person and this book for truly she is in the pages of this document.

Lisa Great

Transforming Lives. Bringing Restoration. Equipping Generations. Impacting People.
Contact information: rdtministries@hotmail.com
Ricky and D'Andrea Thomas
Forever The Witness

Made in the USA
Columbia, SC
09 October 2024

43988018R00043